POETRY OF WONDER

Christian Pascale

Aster Press
Blue Fortune Enterprises, LLC

POETRY OF WONDER
Copyright © 2021 by Christian Pascale.

All rights reserved. Printed in the United States of America. No part of this book may be used or reproduced in any manner whatsoever without written permission except in the case of brief quotations embodied in critical articles or reviews.

This book is a work of fiction. Names, characters, businesses, organizations, places, events and incidents either are the product of the author's imagination or are used fictitiously. Any resemblance to actual persons, living or dead, events, or locales is entirely coincidental.

For information contact :
Blue Fortune Enterprises, LLC
Aster Press
P.O. Box 554
Yorktown, VA 23690
http://blue-fortune.com

Interior and Cover design by Blue Fortune Enterprises LLC, blue-fortune.com
Cover art by Liria Pascale: Morning at the Beach

ISBN: 978-1-948979-71-9
First Edition: September 2021

Dedication

To my wife Liria and my two sons, Raphael and Michel.

Poetry of Wonder is the ideal book for our complicated times. It overflows with the magic of nature, the many faces of love, the lure of exotic places, and the strength of enduring faith. Christian Pascale has a unique voice that resonates equally well with humorous poetry about Gertrude Stein, "a Rose is a Rose," the ethereal flavor of "Autumn Woods," and the poignant love of family in "Her Last Gift." Each poem awakens us to truth while soothing the soul.

Sharon Canfield Dorsey is the author of numerous publications, including poetry books "Walk with Me", "Tapestry", "Captured Moments" and nonfiction books "Daughter of the Mountains" and "Road Trip."

Other titles by Christian Pascale:

Memories Are The Stories We Tell Ourselves
Windows of Heaven

A Hero

A hero's the work of moments,
A daily tapestry of Soul
Not a single one-time reaction
But part of an eternal whole.

Amber Glass

This moment stored in amber glass
an ancient relic from the past.
Will I remember it, and store
within mind's womb, the image spore?

This moment stored in amber glass
A fleeting ghost that soon will pass.
Memory haunting me once more,
Will it withstand time's awful shore?

An Early Fall

Just September, yet fall is in the air.
I feel it in the briskness of the wind
That brings summer's perfume down dark streets.

I smell it in the incense of burning leaves
and the chestnuts roasted by an old man
in the aging Jardin du Luxembourg.

The tourists, like raucous summer birds, screech
along cobblestone streets and Boulevards.
So many tongues, I'll never understand.

For them the rain is soft, the sun is warm.
Almost convinced, I doubt my intuition.
But along the Seine, sunrays are dying.

Paris shakes itself like some large beast
Shedding pastel skin for new, darker hues.
Soft caresses for brusquer advances.

The Parisians move with new intentness.
La rentrée has begun. The race is on.
The leaves will turn golden, and then they will fall.

The tourists march quickly along the Seine.
They're season blind. They scan their calendars.
Autumn is some weeks, a lifetime away.

A Rose is a Rose

That Gertrude Stein, she was so fine.
Too bad she could not write.
She held court but withheld her time
From all the young men she would slight.

That A is A and B is B
Means little to you or me.
A rose is a rose is a rose
Is all she could ever compose.

Autumn Woods

One aging fall in autumn wood
I passed a stream so strong and clear
Which flowed from higher alpine lake
Unblocked by snow that time of year.

When I traced back the downward flow
Of this pure stream so strong and clear
The crystal source to me appeared
Once hid from where I stood below.

I sat before that alpine lake
And when I stooped my thirst to slake
With sky-blue water clear and cold,
I saw my true self never old.

Beachwear

First came the hat man in the flow
Cart with silly summer hats, though
Miss "Sunglasses" next in the row
Preferred her beachwear all aglow.

Up and down the strand, wares in tow,
The beach a stage for daily play.
The actors each in his own way
All played their part till end of day.

The tall black man stood clear away
Fluffy female hat on his head.
Placed in a way it could be said
That he was neither blue nor red.

Then appeared a frizzy-haired child.
Ebony skin and snow-white smile.
Pulled on his shirt, then danced a while
Like a proud princess of the Nile.

Their sale of beachwear nearly done
They vanished in the summer sun
To count the money they had won
From carefree tourists having fun.

Beauty

Beauty is an inner light
Which shines in every smile.
Graced by sweet gentleness
And a certain style.

A breath of concrete innocence
With the fragrance of youth.
A reminder that life is spent
In search of hidden truth.

Belleza

Beauty as the orchid's
Fed by Iguacu falls
And like the jungle's mystery
Your lilting laughter calls.

POETRY OF WONDER

Brazil

Brasilia, "blocos", "apartamentos."
Doomed vision against vaulted sky.
Dystopian design airplane body.
Functional anonymity.
"*Pais do futuro*", always the future.

Rio, bold boisterous beach city
Favelas and fame, samba and sea
Bossa beat, majestic moros
Corcovado, carnival, heaven, hell
Luminous lascivious lady.

Skyscraper stained seething **Sao Paulo.**
Businesses and banks, boutiques and bistros.
Hotels, high-rises, humid highways.
Slums and sushi, New York and Nisei.
Tired traffic, tight taxis, trams and trains.

Bahia, history's squeamish slave port.
White candles floating on the sea.
Mystery, mania, miscegeny.
White and black macumba magic.
Truck trios, slow samba, fast "frevo."

CHRISTIAN PASCALE

Can't Find My Way Home

The horseman urges his mount on
As shadows play in darkening woods,
Leaves yellow-gold which in sun stood
Now menace him with dark night's hood.

He buttons coat against the wind
Pulls fur hat down in night's damp cold.
More miles to go; new day now old.
Twilight's phantoms become more bold.

He whispers to his faithful mount
"You know the way, just take me home.
Far from these woods and obscure gloam.
For I am lost, and we're alone."

And through the fog and rain and snow
His steady stead likes angel's flight
Moves onward, upward through the night
Toward home, hearth, and morning's light.

Church Music

I listen to you touch those keys.
The prelude that you play with ease
Distills your faith in every note.
Your music lifts my thoughts to God.

The peace of prayer your music brings
Calms my thought, my hungry heart sings.
For God's creation, one great whole
United by these chords of Soul.

CHRISTIAN PASCALE

Coming of the Dawn

First, hint of light on onyx night.
Then, like a bud, slowly unfolds,
In subtlety of nascent pink.
It blooms at last in perfect gold.

And in the light's hopeful delight
The day is born. There is no night.
The dark retreats and gives no fight
For nighttime dreams will leave our sight.

The sunlight of our future's dawn
Will purge the sadness of this morn
And clear clean newness like a song
Will sing a promise that is born.

Dandelion Wine

Dandelion wine's so fine
Summer solstice liquor divine.
Flower petals, poor man's wine
Aphrodisiac of ancient time.

Lion's tooth or fairy's clock
Mix with myrrh or apple hops.
Herbal potion precious gold
Orient's elixir of old.

Type of ancient herbal tea
Gluten, sugar, and dairy free.

CHRISTIAN PASCALE

Defender Of The Faith

Are you the thought police
who demand we confess?
And promise us release
Our souls you claim to bless?

And do you check the prayers
Your neighbor says at night?
Butt into his affairs,
Make sure he gets it right?

Control your thoughts that lurk
Like some religious wraith.
Then, let God do his work,
Defender of the faith.

Eternal Rays

Not senile crying in the night
For dying rays of failing light.
Not embers burning once so bright

That sputter out like dimming sight.
Nor stars that fall from Babble's height.
But timeless rays of brilliant light.

CHRISTIAN PASCALE

Expatriate Fall

I miss November's frosty air
Leaves multi-colored by the sun
Like Pilgrim tapestries that run
Down broad New England thoroughfares.

I miss hayrides at a farm,
Red apples at the country fair
The way the sun shines on your hair,
Nantucket's light, its island charm.

I miss Thanksgiving in our style,
Our laughter, Nana in her chair,
Your smile so very like a prayer,
Which warmed me once, a little while.

Fall Color

It is a wonder to behold
When leaves turn orange, red, and gold.
This year we look and wonder why
The leaves are duller, dark and dry.

Some think the cause is lack of rain.
And say it is a crying shame.
I hold past colors in my mind
Unchanged by years or death or time.

CHRISTIAN PASCALE

For Those We Love

I'd like to walk with you today
And take your hand.
It's not this land so far away
That makes me sad.

I take some time to sit and pray.
Distance is just a subtle scheme.
And sadness, ransom we must pay
For lies we choose today to dream.

Fountain Of Youth

The small boy greets the morning sun
With joy, excited with the fun
that he will share with friends who run
through tall wet grass until they're done.

It is no special Christmas day.
He greets each day in the same way.
For each day brings him new uplift.
He cheers, and wonders at its gift.

Like him, let us await each day
With wonder at Life's bold array.
As we begin to see this truth
We too will find our fount of youth.

Ghosts at the Table

I thought that more people would have mourned.
Certainly from our church,
the church he had left to stand for a principle
they no longer considered valid, but sacred to him.

My wife and I revisited his favorite restaurant,
the site of many former after-church lunches
with him and his wife; just the four of us
talking about kids and grandkids. He loved my son deeply.

My wife and I sat in silence thinking about the two empty chairs
across from us at our table, once filled with joy.
The waitress asked about them.
They were her friends, treated her like a daughter.

I saw her wipe the tears from her face when I told her why
he and his wife no longer came.
I had to avert my eyes. My wife started to cry as well.
And so, in silence, we ate with ghosts.

The manager came to our table, his pain evident.
The waitress had told him and he wanted to say how sorry;
"They were really good people," he said. "I hope she is okay."
He wanted to know details and I told him what I could.

POETRY OF WONDER

His wife would get through this, I said. She is with her daughter.
But I did not know if I would. Get through it, that is.
I thought of the years of service he had given our church.
Now, he was mourned by me, my wife, a waitress, and a manager.

The others might write letters, which his wife did not want to read.
I would not write. I had spoken to her. We would speak again.
So I sat at the table and thought what he would say if he were there.
The memories ached. It was just me, my wife, and the ghosts at the table.

Waterfalls

Waterfalls of light
Cascade on time's darker night
Irid, ever bright.

Snow

Tracks scar fallen snow
Once untouched virginity.
Snow will fall again.

CHRISTIAN PASCALE

Winds of the mind

Spring winds blow strongly
Across desert of my mind.
But will they bring rain?

Tokyo

This city does not sleep
She has a promise to keep.
A new dawn to greet.

Orchid

You the orchid wild
Live in dark-green jungle halls
Your mystery calls.

Heaven's Poetry

God speaks to me in poems
So simple and so fine.
They tell me who I am
What is forever mine.

They weave a tapestry
So rich and clear and bold,
Reveal God's artistry
A wonder to behold

Her Last Gift

Not just some antique chair
Or necklace she left there,
Nor silver knives and forks.

In a drawer full of socks
Just an old jewelry box
With a note, very short.

"We'll meet again someday.
Don't ever doubt the way.
There is no need to cry.

If you wonder what I'm doing
Where I am or what I'm viewing,
I'm just eating Blueberry pie.
Love, Mom"

How Many More

How many more lives?
How many mothers now without children?
I want to reach out, touch, and hug them all.

But I cannot hug all.
Too many mothers, too many places.
I pray for them, their children and America.

I pray for God's guidance
To see beyond color, black or white or brown;
To see beyond young, old, male or female.

We're all brothers and sisters
Made in God's image.
Let us live as children of God.

I Have A Promise To Keep

There is a promise I must keep
When through my mind your image creeps.
I promised you I would not weep.

There is a promise I must to keep
When sadness through my mind now sweeps.
Let no regret in my heart seep.

There is a promise I must keep
Life, hope, and love are never cheap.
And what we sow is what we reap.

There is a promise I must keep
When now I lay me down to sleep
And sorrow like a knife cuts deep.

There is a promise I must keep.
Let joy and love in me repeat
I have a promise I must keep.

Into the Light

One day, not so far off
We'll step into the light.
The darkness will have gone
The day, no longer night.

We won't walk alone in silence
Or run and bike so quickly by
But stop, talk, up close, then shake hands
and meet in groups and not ask "why?"

We'll find things at the supermarkets,
Toilet paper, conversation.
We'll dine in restaurants with our friends.
Fear will flee with isolation.

Some will remember just a dream.
We won't forget the fallen. Stay faithful!
In a new time of plenty and health,
Will we remember to be grateful?

CHRISTIAN PASCALE

I Owe Them That (FLORIDA)

Sometimes the pain and fear turn us away.
Easy not to read what the papers say,
Or cry at a family's loss, senseless.
Those twelve, the young, the hopeful, the fearless.

A guard protected the weak, loved coffee.
A college grad worked to help the needy.
A deputy who fly-fished rivulets
With his son ran fearless toward bullets.

A bell will toll now twelve times in dismay.
I cannot fail to read what papers say
About those who died in the bar that day.
I cannot turn away. I owe them that.

In The Rain

I was seven and she was so late.
Waiting, crying at the school's gate,
I thought she left me in the rain.

But she came. Knew I'd been afraid.
She swore she would never again
let me wait crying in the rain.

She waited with me as years passed.
And saw my sons grow up too fast.
Alone with memories amassed

Constant companions in the night.
She then began to lose her sight
Wanted to move on to the light.

I knew that I could not complain
When a Christmas Eve, once again
She left me crying in the rain.

CHRISTIAN PASCALE

In the Dawn's Early Light

In the dawn's early light
our flag still flies
above the bastions of freedom.

It is our flag. It belongs to all of us.
It is red, white, and blue, not Nazi red and black,
Nor anarchist black nor communist red.

It's our symbol, all of ours. It stands for
the valor and sacrifice of patriots, purity of freedom,
the eternally vigilant blood that runs within us.

For we the people stand shoulder to shoulder.
We will not yield to chaos, violence, and terror.
This is our flag. It belongs to the people, to all of us.

Japan

Searching East, I only found West.
In teeming streets, it was all there.
This ultra-modern high-rise kingdom
Once triumphant in tranquility.

Lost among stores, shops, and cafes,
overlooked by the bustling crowd,
obscured by hawking street vendors.
Silence still lives in wooden walls.

La Pucelle D'orleans
Johanne d'Arc 30 May 1431

It's men who've made the rules
and what we learn in schools.
It's politics, perverts, and priests
who brought her death and her defeat.

The English, the French, the same.
One cursed, one praised her name.
Her sins they claimed were three.
She spoke to God, was free.

A witch, wore pants, a heretic.
Delusional schizophrenic.
Her voices and her pageboy hair
made the priests and knights all beware.

They burned her at the stake
Soon the French hearts would ache.
Witch, priestess, headstrong, free.
What have men done to thee.

Late Winter's Promise

The swans are at the lake once more
Like summer's promise long foretold.
Snow angels floating well offshore
On waters deep and dark and cold.

I've waited for them for a year
with hope and joy, a patience thing.
The creatures we all hold most dear
can wake in us eternal spring.

Renewal's hint in their domain;
New cygnets will Spring waters glide.
With timid movements they'll remain
in safety at their mother's side.

These graceful swans reflect, take flight
and rise from lake-side, pure and white.
Their wings flash bright bold blinding light
against the winter's somber night.

Lawrence

Out of wedlock, lost son,
not DH but the other one.
Lawrence of Arabian land
British steel forged in desert sand.

Soldier and spy, his name still rings
in the minds of rebels and kings,
Highwayman with price on his head
Gaining an honor long since dead.

With passion, played his role in time.
served a great empire that was blind,
sensed the future, read all the signs.
Of Arab revolt, he helped prime.

Practicing a once noble trade
honor and heart the choice he made.
Though duty the expected thing
he chose to help that Arab Spring.

Leopard Encaged

Back and forth across his cage
Pacing inches of his rage,
Leopard moves on padded feet
In his silence, he's discrete.

Claws clipped, defenseless sits.
Lost lethargic soul, he fits
the part. Bureaucrat in black
caught in a silent, self-made trap.

Wonders if he will be free
from his cage, he wants to flee.
Eyes like a gunman's for hire
capture me in pools of fire.

CHRISTIAN PASCALE

Loneliness

I don't think I fear death
or maybe not as much as life.
I shall not forget your caress

nor the ache I feel inside.
For what is there to fear in death
when I have known loneliness.

Liria

Time will not change the way I feel
nor seal our love, make it more real.
My heart's now yours and it will be
ever, always, and all for thee.

Loup Garou

On Orleans Isle near old Quebec
In Saint Anne de Beaupre,
I met a pretty girl one day
by night she was a lycanthrope.

By light, she wore a girl's disguise
of amber hair with dark blue eyes.
Who under autumn hunter's moon
sang a werewolf's bloody tune.

Her nails, she painted scarlet red,
were claws and fangs from which I fled.
With teeth so pointed, sharp, and white
she took my beating heart that night.

For those who would go to Orleans Isle
and the town Saint Anne de Beaupre
Beware the wild girl's hungry smile
beneath a blood-red autumn moon.

Mallards

Ducks like tugboats cross the lake.
Sunrays dance upon their wake.
Smokestacks tall of emerald green
As sun's light brings out their sheen

I have seen them there before.
Back then, there were only four.
More have come this summer's end
Farther south, to winter spend.

Perhaps they will stay a while.
Found again like some lost child.
Floating echoes of the past.
Memories that always last.

Mata Atlantica

Within my mind's rich canopy
 I see the jungle green up high
where golden parakeets can fly
above the rocks and deep blue sea.

Blue-yellow parrots sing off key
and screech, "Be on your way," to me.
Tucano, jewel-eyed, in a tree,
banana bill up turned in glee,

knows the tropics belong to him.
The cliffs above the peaceful sea
dare me to glide to sand, and swim
in soothing waters, wild and free.

Within this jungle of my mind
I see reflected for all time
the rainbow-colored tropic sky
that I would dare to versify.

Memory of Sea and Sun

That childhood day floats back to me
from deep within my memory.
A day of sun, and sand, and sea
Where bobbing birds keep near the lee.

Perfumed petunias hold the air
their bright bold colors everywhere.
They line the path down to the beach
that brings soft sand within my reach.

I walk in thought. This summer sand
teases my toes like a lover's hand.
And as I stroll along the strand
the magic seashells fill my pants.

Each shell, each smell, a memory
when I recall both sand and sea
as they were and will always be.
This childhood scene lives on in me.

The sun's rays play upon my breast
like gentle fingers' soft caress.
The deep embrace by this warm light
protects me now against the night.

Mist and Moon

Fog floats over warmer water,
Ascending air caresses night.
Mist maneuvers on life's lake
and softly steals away day's light.

Slender sliver, silvery moon
sails forth across night's darker sea.
Seeking out moon's lonely daughters
who blink so bright eternally.

Monet's Wife, Woman in Garden

He often spends the hours of night
painting the shades of day with brush.
He tries to get the shadows right.
One stroke, the next, he dare not rush.

His mind flies back to afternoon,
the garden's flowers, her soft dress.
The summer light was gone too soon
like memories of her caress.

Music in the Metro

A musician named Bell, Josh Bell
plays million-dollar violin.
Six Bach pieces performed so well
with violin beneath his chin.

He stands there, playing for small change.
Thousands of commuters pass him by.
Few people stop, applaud his strain.
Some passing children wonder why

busy parents drag them away,
as if to shun this concert gift.
For there is never time to stay,
to rest and feel music's uplift.

The hurried adults cannot hear
nor then respond in childlike way.
They cannot take the gift, that's clear,
this magic music played today.

My Lady of the Night

I will wait by candlelight
for my "lady of the night."
Near my mirror, in my chair,
she will find me waiting there.

Other women can't compare.
Rousing beauty, hers so rare.
Be she dark or be she fair,
she will find me waiting there.

Under moonshine burning bright,
I now embrace this welcomed tryst.
Be it wrong or be it right,
she will come to me tonight.

CHRISTIAN PASCALE

My Son

I saw my son the other day,
the man he has become.
For he is such a gentle soul
life's battle he has won.

Computer games he finds a treat
with people, he is shy.
He shuns things where you must compete
and that, I think, is why

he does not care for clothes or cars
nor worldly charms' caress.
You won't find him in clubs or bars,
he walks in quietness.

New Dawn

The dew sits softly on the ground
in silent stillness, there's no sound.
The birds have still to come awake,
for it is just before daybreak.

I sit, wait for the rising sun
For this I know, that it will come
and warm the earth, the birds will sing,
their song a new beginning bring.

It is a perfect time for prayer
to know that peace is everywhere.
It must come now just like the dawn
in innocence of the new morn.

CHRISTIAN PASCALE

Now And Then

When I was young, I wished I'd be
much older than the younger me.
So I could travel, fall in love;
do things older life's made of.

As years went by, I wished I'd be
much younger than the older me;
then I would travel, fall in love,
do things younger life's made of.

Then one bright day it came so clear
no chains of hour, or day, or year.
I'll always be, just now, just me.
Not young, not old, eternity.

Nursery Rhyme

The cup has the saucer,
the knife has the fork.
And laps have napkins
to keep the food off.

The chair has the table
its legs don't have feet.
But who will I find
to rock me to sleep?

The earth has the rain,
the sun has its heat.
But whom will I find
to rock me to sleep?

Then whom will I find
to rock me to sleep,
to say me a prayer
my sweet soul to keep?

CHRISTIAN PASCALE

Odysseus

By Circe's lair, he hears a sound.
The drops of silence trickling down
leave him spellbound, tied to the spot,
like moss that clings to rugged rock.

He dare not find a way to leave
caught in the web his lover weaves.
He dreads the chaos freedom brings,
can't shed this peace for braver things.

He sends an ant out on a twig
with leaf as sail, square-rigged brig.
This tiny helmsman heeds not fears,
the raging waters bravely steers.

The pygmy pilot lets him see
that all of nature must live free.
Bewitched by false tranquility,
he knows escape must be the key.

He leaves his men locked in their cell
lost in the perfumes of her spell.
For he must go, he has a home
and cannot leave his wife alone.

Painting Reality

She paints with brush. I sketch in words
the things we saw, the sounds we heard.

The magic dancing in the light
the break of dawn, the end of night.

These vivid colors, words akin
unfold reality within.

Passing of a Friend

How is it my heart did not feel
the sudden silence so surreal?
Why didn't I see, why didn't I know,
what I should have sensed months ago?

Waiting for news that never came.
Searching obits for your name.
Trying, never completed a call
shock, finality of it all.

The emptiness I now conceal
pretending your death isn't real.
You're on some trip, you'll soon be back.
It's easy to avoid the fact.

It will take me some time to heal;
my broken heart's not made of steel.
You could have told me you would go
before you left me lone and low.

Path of Light

The light rays dance upon the lake
that shimmers, touched by setting sun.
The mallards leave behind their wake
paddling home when the day is done.

As if a road straight to my door,
the sun's reflection follows me.
And water that was dark before
glows white like wave caps of the sea.

Pentagram

Her eyes burned cold, red light, and lust.
She scratched a sign upon the sand
with witch's rod. She spoke and sprinkled dust
from hallowed ground on firebrands.

Across the flames she drew her hand,
invoked black demons out of hell.
A tempest came at her command,
the sound like peals from death's church bell.

The fire's legacy of ash
was cooled by rain that swept the land.
And she alone remained steadfast,
still safe inside her Pentagram.

Petunias 1982

Sun lifts up these simple flowers
that sit so proud on my back deck.
Wait in their boxes for night's breeze
to come extract their smell with ease.

A perfumed path of endless hours;
memories of summer's striptease
smell of ocean, taste of sand.
Dreams once deserted on the strand.

Present and Future

If present is past, it won't last
time flies by so very fast.
The future, present's obscure view,
and hindsight, just a sad review

Of all the things we wished we knew,
the present never has a clue.
Present is just future's past
but hope in good is all that lasts.

Quarantine

Fear can't separate us, both you and me.
Looking through ever clear windows of time
from the other side of the street or world,
we wave at each other's smiling faces.

We can never touch but still we can talk
over our cell phones and computers.
We share our love, our commonality
for we are still all brothers and sisters.

I won't let a disease isolate me,
quarantine my body, never my mind.
It cannot keep you and I from caring.
It can't keep us from being who we are.

CHRISTIAN PASCALE

Rachel

One fall morning in crisper air
I left in search of memory.
Wondering "Is my love still there,"
still in Montreal, in Canada.

A Quebec song played in my head
as I drove north and back through time;
words of French poets long since dead
sung by a girl who once was mine.

I slept that night not in her bed
but in a somber cold motel.
Ring on her finger broke the spell
of warmer days and what we'd said.

It was cold as I drove home
by myself, very much alone.
Heading into the winter wind
with only dreams of where I'd been.

A Rendezvous with Life

My rendezvous with Life not Death.
No dark, violent, battered hill.
I choose the light with every breath,
I hear your voice and I am still.

Barricades of time, not mine,
I will not make that rendezvous.
When spring comes round bright flowers fine,
then will I turn my thoughts to you.

Your apple blossoms fill the air
a contrast to pandemic war.
My hope's in your eternal care
a rendezvous with Death no more.

Scanning the Daybreak Sky

Like data virus scan, my mind
searches the new dawn's daybreak sky
looking for storm warnings that come
like dark clouds before a cold rain.

Problems consort with new mornings
flowing into day, hour by hour.
Please give me the strength to meet them.
Where is the night's tranquility?

A night hymn playing in my head
takes me to its pure still waters,
to peaceful greener pastures.
With Your help, I can change this day.

Seasons

Soft summer's light slowly fades
and trades pastel for darker shades
of amber autumn moon's dark night.

The winter's darkness now descends
and shorter days eclipse the light
till spring's rebirth and winter ends.

CHRISTIAN PASCALE

September Day in July

September's day within my mind
is trapped somehow in this July.
As the rain clouds fill the sky,
my body sweats. I wonder why.

September's trapped in this July.
As jailor clouds bring waves of heat,
the scented flowers sickly sweet
touch humid soil beneath my feet.

The jailor clouds and waves of heat
deny that cool September song.
I hope that it won't be too long
till fall is here and summer's gone.

Stephan Bennett's Beautiful Sky

Your song plays softly in my head.
It flows from touching magic strings.
You give life to those strings once dead.
I come alive, my heart now sings.

Your music brings me needed peace
from tired time, I find release.
I touch the sky; unfold my wings.
My heart is filled with better things.

Star Traveler

Star traveler
heading for a sun.
Star traveler
when the day is done

Out into the darkness
looking for the light.
Star traveler
crossing endless night.

Out into the night
looking for the light

The ship is turning
spinning like your mind
at the beginning.
The end you will find.

Stay in the moment
Dreams wind round your mind
Life is a circle,
far beyond all time.

POETRY OF WONDER

Out into the night
looking for the light

Star traveler,
heading for a sun.
Star traveler,
when the day is done.

Star traveler,
heading for a sun.
Star traveler,
when the day is done.

CHRISTIAN PASCALE

Succubus

At night, when sleep is far away,
when mist and fog obscure the bay,
I hear a strange sound, soft not loud
too sweet to be from thundercloud.

I lie undressed upon the bed,
 a phantom vamp inside my head,
A priestess, succubus of night
I can't resist her warm invite.

I know her presence made of dreams
arousal in the night it seems.
From daylight's dawn, demons must flee.
Reality is what we see.

Tango

Her spiked heels twist and turn in step
through strides, cross steps, pirouettes.
Two bodies move across the floor,
they slide, then step, then slide once more.

Forward, then back, they move with grace.
His hands control her slender waist.
His fingers lightly touch her spine
then lead her through the tango line.

Advance again slide right this time,
then back, point toes, oh so sublime.
She spins around him with her charms
supported by caressing arms.

His eyes on hers, two bodies one,
seduction's game is almost done.
They play their roles, part and blend.
The dance of love comes to an end.

Technology And Time Machines

I detest travel in planes.
I much prefer the time of trains.
They sat in dining cars to eat
and there was room to stretch your feet.

If I believed in time machines
I'd fly back to that time of dreams
where lullaby of churning wheels
brought peaceful sleep and gourmet meals.

I'd take a liner, cross the sea.
Play paddleball on decks, with glee
Go to masked balls aboard the ship
and dance the tango hip to hip.

I could spend much more time with books
and not get all those weird, strange looks
when I don't read from my new Nook.
I might just stop and learn to cook.

Back then computers did not rule
the internet was not a tool.
An instant gratification,
I'd rather take a vacation!

POETRY OF WONDER

I miss bookstores' musty smells
and conversation's many spells.
Some time to perch, drink herbal tea
or watch the birds sit on a tree.

We tweet, text, use social media
rent hotel rooms on Expedia.
We never have to speak at all.
The written word is now a scrawl.

Past centuries still beckon me,
then we had real liberty.
Tech giants will say we're all much freer.
Technology's our panacea.

If I could find a time machine,
I would go back to where we've been.

CHRISTIAN PASCALE

The Country

I weave for you a crown of red roses,
And marigolds bunched with white corn cockle.
Then you, adorned in cotton and lace,
bleached white by the sun's great golden face,

kick off your street shoes and shake loose your head.
We walk cold summer's shores of alpine lakes.
We talk till the sun turns a lipstick red,
as the night and the stars make my heart ache.

The moon illumines dark mauve mountains
as the waves lap so softly on the shore.
Frogs croak longing lullaby's from fountains,
and the moths brush so bravely at our door.

In the morning light, three timid puppies,
Skin soft as satin, awake to the dawn.
They run and jump to lick our warm faces
then roll round and round, dew fresh on the lawn.

We search, then pick and eat what nature yields
from bright berry bushes in wild wet fields.
The city seems so far away.
 I think we'll stay another day.

The Dry Season

The dry season has come to us again
as grass turns browner, smoke is in the air.
Day-thoughts fill up with dust. There is no rain.
Even the rivers seem swallowed by sun.

We draw and drink from a deep well for days.
Like the sweet nectar of Life that bees find,
inspiration's clear drops bring growth in ways
so nothing can stop the beauty that comes

In our thought-garden. Bud then full flower
blooming despite dryness in this parched land.
Like flowers, we drink Life fully each hour
til the rain comes and dry season is done.

CHRISTIAN PASCALE

The Healer

Like a small pebble gently tossed
into the world's lake,
your prayer ripples my consciousness.
From dreams, I awake.

My heart a kite to wind unfurled
rejoices at your prayer.
With Spirit's updraft I can rise
from seascape into air.

The Hummingbird

The hummingbird has come at last
to slake his thirst and end his fast.
A buzz, a swoosh, emerald green
this visit's part of his routine.

If I don't put his nectar out
at my window, he'll come to pout.
He'll make me feel just like a lout
of this, I'm sure, I have no doubt.

When I retrieve his water jar,
he'll buzz my head, he's so bizarre.
He is a very selfish one;
fights all the other birds that come.

But I put up with all his tricks
ensuring to my yard he sticks.
I would not have him go away
for it is he that makes my day.

CHRISTIAN PASCALE

The Irishman and His English Lady

Highwayman to his lady fair,
"Let's sail the moon to far-off lands."
He raised his lips to kiss her hands
as scent of jasmine filled the air.

"This galleon moon on cloudy sea
will carry us on new sun's tide.
Say 'yes,' and be my bonnie bride.
Oh come, then come away with me."

"And where shall we go, handsome sir?
"The dogs will hunt you like a deer."
"No, soon we'll get away from here,"
said the Éire, smiling up at her.

The story's told as years go by.
In bigot bars, hate still holds sway
though chauvinists may rule the day.
Let us never let true love die.

The Journey

On silver wings across the sea
I fled my mediocrity,
this endless fogging in my head.
I went in search of life instead.

I searched for jobs, I tried to write,
and in the darkness of the night
I walked in dreams through crowded streets
past wishful women's well-lit seats.

I talked, I loved, I cried, and fled.
When daylight found me in my bed,
I rose and searched again, you see.
Until I finally found me.

The Language of the Flowers

A fairy once taught me how to
speak the language of the flowers.
"They'll whisper silly things to you,"
he said. "I listen by the hours.

"They talk of sun and rain and snow
Of bees and birds and night and day.
Their lives seem much like ours, you know
but not care-filled," said the fay.

My fairy friend then spoke again
sipping nectar from a flower.
"But they're different from us when
We watch them close in their bower.

"They do not toil, they do not spin.
They bask in coolness not in sin.
And do not fight nor try to win.
but simply drink the pure light in."

The Poet

Painting with words, he wields his brush.
Fills with his pen the empty page.
Visual colors, sounds, tastes and smells
Like siren's songs or scent of sage

which capture hues of memory.
The magic words, no hint of age,
evoke people, places. They tell
stories on an ever-changing stage.

CHRISTIAN PASCALE

The Sea of Faith

Our sea of faith still strong, still full.
Not mist, nor fog, nor watered dreams
that drown our hopes in salted squill,
though life is rarely what it seems.

Can we be true to each other?
As we sit on life's cold beach
watch tides, our lives recover.
Yet often peace seems out of reach.

As we protest for what is right
And love within our hearts now beats
where ignorant armies clashed by night
children's laughter will fill our streets.

The Seed or the Flower

Seed or flower, which is first?
When was it, their primordial birth?
Was the seed the first in time's line?
Did flower come before in time?

The seed contains all that it needs
to grow, unfold, to bloom, to shine.
Flowers attract the busy bees
True creation is found in Mind.

Flower or seed, which one came first
Flower's idea or seed's birth?
The flower is the seed's new dress
The seed holds the flower's promise.

CHRISTIAN PASCALE

The Verdelak

This creature of the darkest night
he cannot tolerate the light
nor feel the warm, nurturing sun.
By truth he's doomed, cursed to run.

I see his undead, putrid flesh
Das Capital in spades expressed.
A soldier of autocracy
he feeds on our democracy.

He promises all truth in sight,
this creature of the endless night.
With fangs he'll pierce and suck your soul
your lifeless body now drained whole.

He has no life, he has no creed
but money, self, and endless greed.
And if you meet him watch your back
for you should fear this verdelak.

Waves

As waves of light, not of the sea
need no molecules to be,
as photons of pure energy.
Like them we shine refulgent, free.

In Spirit's brilliant beams of light,
darkness disappears, instant flight.
Suffused with Soul-borne lambency,
effulgent, we, His symmetry.

CHRISTIAN PASCALE

When I Saw You Waiting

Across the many miles I saw
you hungry, waiting at my door
for food, I thought. But no, much more!
For peace, for Life, your country's too.

I wonder just what I would do
in insane heat on desert floor
or winds of war on monsoon shore.
Your courage warms my heart, much more.

Sick, wounded, dead, I've seen the gore,
and children thirsty for what's due
which never comes but for a few
who leave their home for something new.

But this I know and this is true:
Despite sickness, famine, and war,
God's love is yours and was before
you stood there waiting at my door.

Wisteria Bones

Wisteria vine in my yard grows
Cascading drops, mauve orchestra.
Entwined around the pergola

Grape-like clusters on the vine.
The lilac petals' pungent smell
and fading fragrance soon repel.

With blossoms withered by the light,
amethyst then turns to gray with
rancid smell, a poisonous white.

Like death's pale veil in mournful dirge
a funeral in floral flight
wisteria's beached bones now emerge.

Within Not Shut-in

Remaining behind our closed doors,
Pesach Israelites of yore,
we too wait for the plague to pass.

Like them, we paint our innocence,
Lamb's blood, on every mental door.
Fasting from fear, courage restored.

No wilderness of doubt and death.
We walk in Love in every place
and know that where we are is safe.

We live in heaven's sacred home
embracing always the stillness
which our lives and others' will bless.

Wizard

Were I a wise wizard of old,
I would bewitch you with my spell.
I'd break into your dreams so bold
that chain you in your prison cell.

I would dare ten thousand demons
and all the shrieking fiends of hell.
If you'd love me for this season,
I'd hold you tight, your fears I'd quell.

Acknowledgements

As far as I can remember I have always written poetry. During my early years, I wrote many poems which remained in dusty drawers over the years. It was not until I joined the James City poets in Tidewater Virginia that I was able to hone my craft and find my voice. Any success this book may have is due to the advice given by members of this group of poets. I would like to single out Sharon Canfield Dorsey for her friendship and for her kind review of this book

I want to thank my two sons, Michel and Raphael, and my wife, Liria for their love and support. My wife's painting is featured on the cover art and she has been a sounding-board for all my poetry.

I deeply appreciate the help of my editor and publisher, Narielle Living, without whose encouragement and advice this book never would have come to fruition.

ABOUT THE AUTHOR

Christian Pascale is a writer and a poet who was born in Brooklyn, New York. He graduated from Lafayette College Magna Cum Lauda with degrees in French and International Relations. At Lafayette, he was inducted into the Phi Beta Kappa honor society and then went on to receive an M.A. in European Area Studies from American University in Washington D.C. and a Doctorat de l'université from La Sorbonne in Paris, France. During his early years, he worked as a substitute teacher, a tennis instructor in Europe and the U.S., a teacher of English as a Foreign Language, a political fundraiser, and Director of Studies at a New England preparatory school. For more than thirty years, he worked in both domestic and foreign assignments for the United States Government.

Christian has published twenty poems in two internationally distributed magazines and is currently a member of the James City Poets. He is married to Liria Hoffmann Pascale who is a native Brazilian and an architect. They live in Williamsburg, Virginia and have two adult sons.

He can be found at christianpascale.com.